SCHOLASTIC

Elementary English

Course Book 3

Published by Scholastic India Pvt. Ltd.
A subsidiary of Scholastic Inc., New York, 10012 (USA).
Publishers since 1920, with international operations in Canada, Australia, New Zealand, the United Kingdom, India, and Hong Kong.

For information regarding permission, write to:
Scholastic India Pvt. Ltd.
A-27, Ground Floor, Bharti Sigma Centre
Infocity-1, Sector 34, Gurgaon (Haryana) 122001
Email: education@scholastic.co.in

Typeset at Digital Expressions

First edition: 2009
Reprint: 2009, March 2010, 2011 (twice), 2012, 2014, 2016, 2019, 2021, 2023, 2025

ISBN-13: 978-81-8477-356-9

Contents

S. No.		Language Development				
S. No.	Chapters	Reading Comprehension	Vocabulary	Spelling	Grammar	Punctuation
1	We Are One World (Poem)	Questions and answers	Identifying images of famous landmarks	Difference in pronunciation of 's', 'c', 'sc' words	Common and proper nouns	
2	Best Friends (Story)	Questions and answers	Different jobs/ Choosing the correct word	Fill in the blanks ('s', 'c', 'sc')	Singular and plural	Capital words, full stops, question marks, exclamation marks and commas
3	After the Rain (Story)	Questions and answers	Collective nouns	Different sounding 'oo' words	Classifying nouns into names, places, things	Correcting the punctuation
4	Feelings (Poem)	Questions and answers	Movement of animals	Fill in the blanks with 'oo' words	Helping words	
5	Rumours (Story)	Questions and answers	Odd word out	Different sounding 'ea' words	Past tense	Capital letters/Exclamation marks
6	The First Earnings (Biography)	Questions and answers	Contractions of words	Words with 'ie' and 'ei'/Rhyming words	Using 'not'	Correcting the punctuation
7	Saving Grandma's Tree (Story)	Questions and answers	Opposite words	Choosing the correct word	Adjectives	Correcting the punctuation
8	The Swing (Poem)	Questions and answers	Synonyms	Using 'u' and 'ou'	Adjectives of degree	
9	The Stick That Grew Shorter (Story)	Questions and answers	Homophones	Using 'gh'	Possessive nouns	Correcting the punctuation
10	SOS! Let's Recycle! (Non-fiction)	Questions and answers	Pairs of words	Homophones–choosing the correct option	Adverbs	Rewriting sentences as slogans
11	Fishing (Poem)	Questions and answers	Unscrambling words and matching with pictures	Choosing the correct homophone	Adverbs	
12	Moving Away (Story)	Questions and answers	Using prefixes to make opposite words	Using 'o' and 'au'	Pronouns	Correcting the punctuation
13	Outer Space (Poem)	Questions and answers	Suffixes	Using 'bt' and 'pt'	Prepositions	
14	Time to Hibernate (Play)	Questions and answers	Similes	Adjectives with 'tious' and 'ious'	Sentences–imperative, statement, question	

Communication Skills			Social Skills	Fun Time
Writing	Listening*	Speaking	Everyday English	Activity
Looking at a picture and describing it	Counting the number of adjectives in a passage	Talking about a recent trip	Using time words	Locating countries on a political map
Jobs of parents	Naming people doing the jobs described	Speaking about a naughty child you know	Discussing daily routine	Words beginning with 'be'
Fill in the blanks	Following instructions for actions	Talking about life as an insect	Ordering food	Adding letters to 'one' and making new words
Movie review	Tongue twister	Describing a favourite movie	Buying clothes	Back to front
A 'thank you' letter	Guessing answers to riddles	Sharing jokes or riddles in class	Making up a joke	Quiz
Ways for children to add to the family income	Listening to a conversation and answering the questions	Reciting your favourite poem	Interacting with a visitor	Finding out about Rameswaram and Ram Navmi
Writing questions to the answers	Listening to instructions and drawing	Using 'I could', 'I should', 'I would'	Saying goodbye	Finding out about soil erosion and its prevention
Invitation to a birthday party	Identifying missing words from a list you hear	Talking about pets	Describing a classmate	Things you see from a swing
Writing the story as the zamindar	Rewriting dictated sentences	Discussing hobbies	Asking for permission	Words with same letters
Describing your best friend	Listening to sentences and noting the homophones	Past tense	Clarifying information	Making a poster on recycling
Letter to grandparents	Listening and noting down pairs of opposite words	Describing a place you visited recently	Taking a message in a telephone conversation	Naming and colouring sea creatures
Writing a letter to a friend about a new place	Listening to descriptions and identifying things	Rules you follow at home	Disagreeing politely	Listing the changes the boys will experience in Shimla
Describing the night sky	Listening to words and identifying the odd one	Talking about things in nature	Talking about your family	Finding out about Pluto
Writing about hibernating animals	Listening to descriptions and identifying animals	Talking about your favourite season	Interviewing your partner	Making five words using 'HIBERNATE'

*Listening texts on page 117.

Introduction

Elementary English is a complete, practical and easy-to-teach course aimed at students learning English for the first time. While the first few years of the child's life may be spent interacting with parents, siblings and friends who speak the child's mother tongue; as soon as the child is exposed to school and friends of different cultural backgrounds, and starts interacting with media, such as television and computer games, he/she needs to gain fluency in English – the language that dominates most social spheres. This interaction primarily involves listening, speaking and oral communication. In India especially, we have the unique situation that a lot of people who can read and write English very competently are uncomfortable with oral communication. *Elementary English* ensures that every student who uses the books will emerge adept at communicating in English.

Comprising course books, workbooks, audio CDs and teacher manuals, the approach follows the current CBSE, ICSE and major State Boards curriculum. The pedagogical principles followed are designed to encourage participatory learning and collaborative practices. The books have been created by a panel of eminent authors, school and college teachers, and experienced children's publishers.

The *Elementary English* series has been designed to cover the essential skills of the language:

Language development:	**Communication skills:**	**Social and other skills:**
Reading comprehension	Writing	Everyday English
Vocabulary	Listening	Activity
Grammar	Speaking	
Spelling		
Punctuation		

Some of the unique features of *Elementary English* are:

The selection of texts
Each book contains an interesting mix of short stories, poems, plays, speeches, biographies and non-fiction articles on varied subjects. The texts selected are both classic and contemporary so that students are introduced to different styles of writing.

Illustrations in diverse styles
Each text is illustrated in a style appropriate to its contents with paintings, pencil sketches, collages or photographs to encourage the child's aesthetic appreciation of different kinds of art.

Encouragement to understand and analyse
The reading comprehension sections are a combination of inference questions designed to make the child read the text closely, and critical response questions that encourage the child to think and analyse character, situation, moral values and ideas.

Learning through practice
Each lesson contains challenging vocabulary and grammar sections. The grammar exercises are contextualised to contribute meaningfully to children's written and verbal abilities.

Reinforcing concepts
A recap of grammar and vocabulary concepts and terms ensures that old lessons are reinforced at every level and the child's recollection of concepts is refreshed before he or she embarks on new and more challenging exercises.

Speaking and listening exercises
These sections are designed to help students communicate in English with correct pronunciation. Supplementary material is provided in the accompanying audio CD. The activities motivate students to use English in conversation naturally and improve diction.

Writing exercises
Elementary English has sections that will help students develop independent writing skills. Level-appropriate activities stimulate and encourage students to plan, expand and proofread their work.

Everyday English
This is a unique forum where students can apply the language to interact in day-to-day activities. Simple exercises help students to confidently speak in English, and learn the vocabulary and expressions appropriate for common life experiences.

Fun-filled activities
These sections introduce children to entertaining and creative craft projects, crosswords, word games, logic and reasoning games and so on. Although presented as games, these exercises are a vital part of the learning process and help children learn essential language skills.

Acquiring tools for independent learning
The children are taught to use the dictionary and thesaurus (in classes 3, 4 and 5), to do basic research individually or in groups, and to present reports, all of which are independent learning skills crucial for middle and senior school.

Teachers' manual
The teachers' manual with each book contains teaching ideas, strategies and resource material. Along with answers for the exercises, teachers are also provided with pronunciation guides, word meanings and additional information on all the chapters.

Audio CD*
For each chapter in each book, the audio CD provides material for the following sections:
- Reading the text with the proper inflections and pauses
- Pronunciation guide to direct the students on how key words are pronounced
- Spellings, to alert the students to how words are spelt correctly
- Listening, where students have to do exercises based on what they hear
- Speaking, where the students are given a model way of speaking and then encouraged to practice
- Everyday English, where children listen to sample conversations and practice

The audio CD can be used in class and at home for additional practice or in the language lab to focus on oral communication.

Workbook
Each book comes with a workbook, which contains additional exercises to complement and supplement the material in the course books.
With an understanding of the age-appropriate rules and elements that govern English, *Elementary English* will help students to communicate correctly and effectively. The series is designed to make first-generation learners proficient in the language.

**Refer to the audio CD when you see this icon in the course book.*

1 We Are One World

Pierre lives in Canada,
Marla lives in Spain.
But both like to ride their bikes
Along the shady lane.

Liv lives in Norway,
Ramon is in Peru.
But both laugh with the giraffe
When visiting the zoo.

Anwar is Egyptian,
Kim is Japanese.
But both run beneath the sun
And fly kites in the breeze.

Jack is from the U.S.A.,
Karintha is from Chad.
But both can write a poem at night
Upon a writing pad.

Children live all over,
The world's a giant ball.
But far and near, it's very clear
We're one world after all.

---

breeze: a light wind
writing pad: lined sheets of paper fastened at one end and used for writing

Reading Comprehension

Answer the questions.

1. What do Pierre and Marla both like to do?
2. What do Liv and Ramon do at the zoo?
3. What do both Anwar and Kim enjoy doing?
4. What do Jack and Karintha do at night?
5. What is the poet trying to tell us in this poem?

Vocabulary

Read the clues and identify the famous landmarks.

1. Tomb of a Mughal empress in Agra.

   ____

2. These were built as tombs for the kings or Pharaohs of Egypt. ______________

3. The clock tower of the British parliament building in London.

____

4. A statue in New York showing a woman holding up a torch in her hand. It was a gift of friendship from the people of France. ___________

5. This wall in China was built by the emperors to keep the enemy out.

____

6. A victory tower in New Delhi. _______

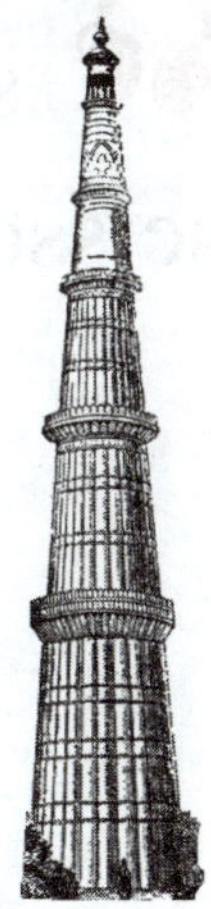

7. An office building in New York that held the record for the tallest building in the world for over forty years after it was built.________________

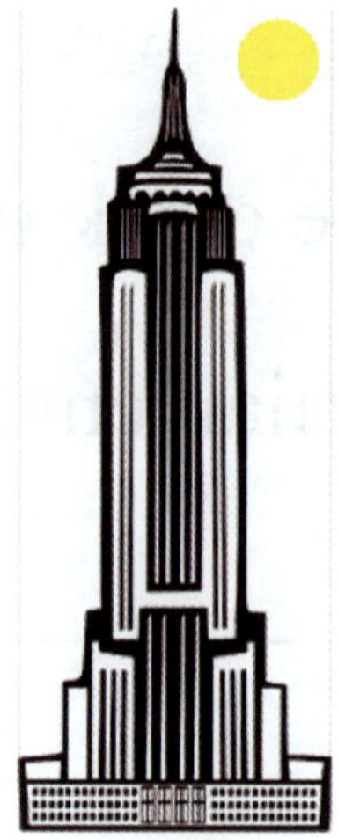

8. A tower in Paris made entirely of iron. ______________

Spelling

Read these words aloud. Notice the difference in pronunciation.

scent cement soft serve September centre scene cell scissors score science scythe scale scepter scooter scarf

Grammar

A **common noun** names any person, animal, place or thing.

A **proper noun** names a specific person, animal, place or thing.

Circle the common nouns in green and the proper nouns in red.

As I sat after school, doing my homework, I heard the doorbell ring. I opened the door to find my partner, Amit, standing outside. He looked very excited and happy. I called him in and asked what had happened.

"Sonya, do you know the entire class is going to Agra to see the Taj Mahal?" he asked.

"No, I have not heard about this trip. Who told you?" I asked Amit, getting as excited as he was.

"Our class teacher, Miss Sharma, told my mother. She says we will go for the weekend and stay overnight at a guest house. She says we will also visit Fatehpur Sikri."

"I must ask my mother for permission," I said as I rushed out of the room.

Writing

Look at this picture and describe what you see.

Listening

Count the number of adjectives you hear.

Speaking

Talk to your partner about a journey to an exciting place. Take turns to be the traveller and the reporter interviewing him/her.

Everyday English

Using time words

When talking about time we use the phrases a quarter to, a quarter past and half past. Talk to your partner about your afternoon and evening schedule using time words.

Activity

Locate the countries named in the poem on this map.

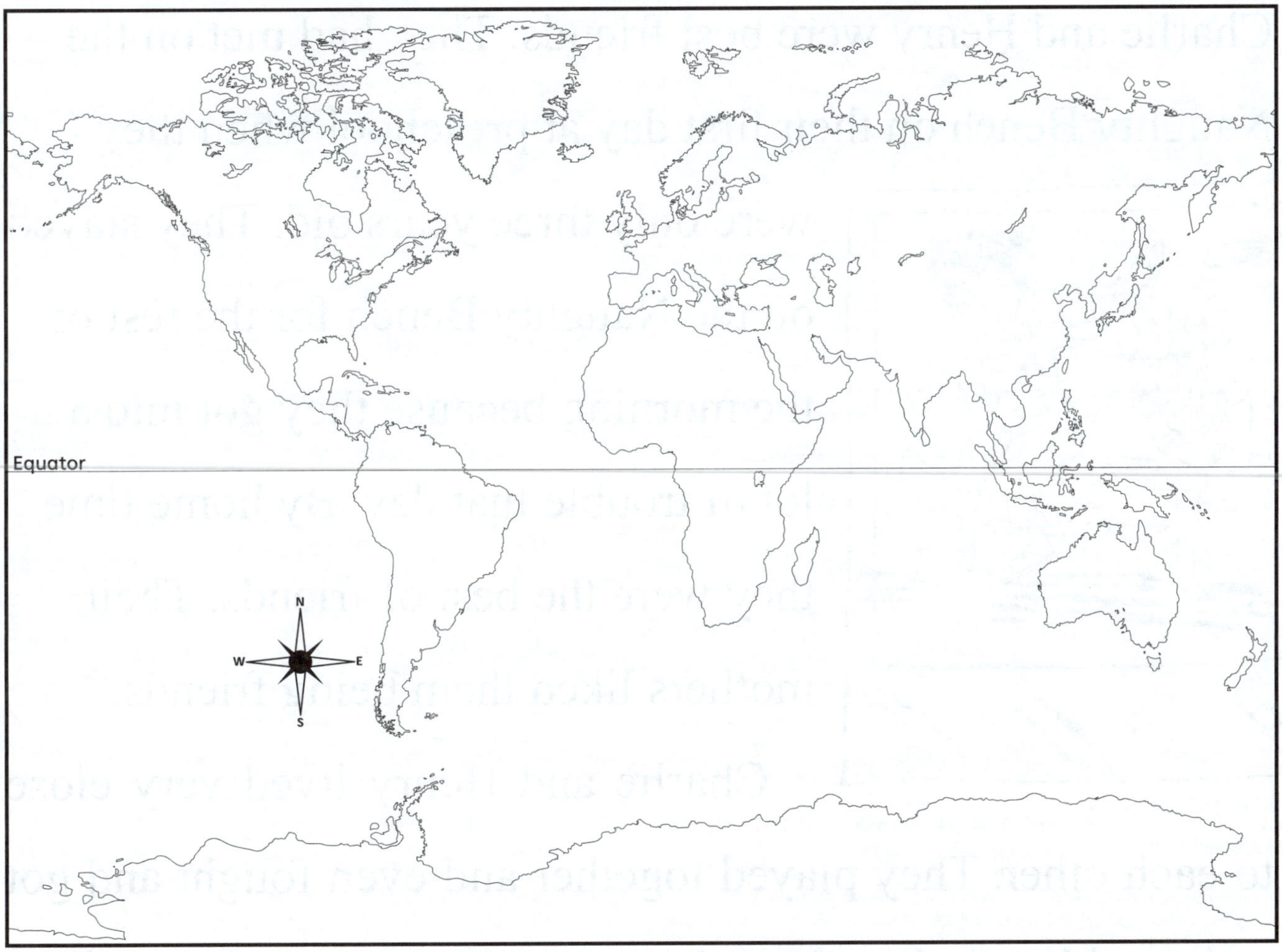

2 Best Friends

Hilary McKay

Charlie and Henry were best friends. They had met on the Naughty Bench on their first day at preschool when they

were only three years old. They stayed on the Naughty Bench for the rest of the morning because they got into a lot of trouble that day. By home time they were the best of friends. Their mothers liked them being friends.

Charlie and Henry lived very close to each other. They played together and even fought and got into trouble together. Soon they were doing almost everything together: haircuts, shoe-shopping and more. They even got sick together.

Naughty Bench: a place where badly behaved children are asked to sit in school
preschool: a school for children between ages two and four

One summer they discovered a wasp's nest together and poked it with sticks until they were simultaneously attacked.

When they started school, their mothers hugged each other in relief. The teacher decided not to separate them and gave them a special table very close to her desk. She said, "I might as well keep all the trouble together." One day, she asked the boys, "How would you two like to be the donkey in our class play?" Charlie and Henry jumped with joy and surprise. The two best friends played the part very well. "Perfect casting," thought the teacher.

---

wasp: a black and yellow flying insect that can sting
simultaneously: at the same time
relief: a feeling of happiness when something unpleasant does not happen

Reading Comprehension

Answer the questions.

1. Where did Charlie and Henry meet?
2. Why were they both on the Naughty Bench?
3. Where did they live and what did they do together?
4. Did they continue to be friends when they went to school?
5. Where did they sit in class?
6. What role did they both perform in the class play?
7. Which words tell you that the teacher was happy with her choice of roles for Henry and Charlie?

Vocabulary

Different people do different jobs. Find the names of some common jobs that are hidden in the word jumble.

I design houses.

I cook food in a hotel or restaurant.

I cut hair.

I act in a movie or a play.

I take the sheep to graze.

I bake cakes and cookies.

b	b	l	q	t	c	h	e	f	f
a	a	c	t	o	r	s	r	d	g
k	r	j	a	q	e	x	k	s	h
e	b	s	h	e	p	h	e	r	d
r	e	h	f	v	n	c	q	w	l
a	r	c	h	i	t	e	c	t	k
e	c	v	b	m	n	t	y	o	p

Fill in the blanks with the correct endings to make new words.

1. arm ____________________ chair/noon
2. match ____________________ port/box
3. egg ____________________ shell/stick
4. foot ____________________ field/ball
5. butter ____________________ fly/sun

Spelling

Fill in the blanks with s, c or sc words.

1. These roses have a wonderful ________.

2. _______ hardens as it dries.

3. Her hands were _______ and small.

4. The waitress welcomed us with a _______.

5. ________ is the ninth month in the year.

6. This chocolate has a soft ________.

Grammar

Singular means one of something and **plural** means more than one. You can convert nouns from singular to plural by adding **-s, -es, -ies** or **-ves**.

Give plural forms of the words by adding -s, -es, -ies and -ves.

knife	____________	bush	____________
army	____________	dog	____________
wolf	____________	uniform	____________
strawberry	____________	leaf	____________
wife	____________	glass	____________
loaf	____________	church	____________

Punctuation

Capital letters are used for the first word in a sentence, the first spoken word in a dialogue and proper names.

Full stops are used at the end of statements and commands.

Question marks are used at the end of questions.

Exclamation marks are used to end exclamations.

Commas are used for short pauses, to separate items in a list and to separate spoken and unspoken words.

Rewrite the sentences using the correct punctuation.

1. where shall we go for the holidays

____

2. would you like to eat something

____

3. where is your scarf

____

4. how are you feeling today

____

5. this cake is delicious

____

6. it is time for the movie

____

7. may i please borrow your pencil

____

8. when will the bell ring

____

9. it is a hot day

____

Writing

Complete the sentences to describe your mother's or your father's job. You may use the following words.

office hospital car bus home bank hardworking clever tired happy

My ____________ is a ________________________________.

He/she ____.

He/she works in a ____________________________________.

What he/she likes about the job is

____.

Listening

Listen to the description of some jobs and name the person who does each job.

Speaking

Do you know anyone like Charlie or Henry—two little boys who are always in trouble?

Tell the class about some naughty child you know.

Everyday English

Discussing daily routine

Discuss your daily routine with your partner.

Activity

To be or not to be

All the words below begin with be.

Write the full word that matches the meaning.

be________ you sleep in it

be________ an insect

be________ it rings

be________ a vegetable

be________ to start

be________ a large, hairy animal

be________ a small fruit

3 After the Rain

One day after it rains, go to the garden or a park. Look closely at the dirt. You may see an earthworm. Earthworms come out of the dirt after the rain.

The earthworm is funny. It does not have arms or legs or bones. It cannot make noise. It does not have ears or nose or teeth.

---

dirt: earth or soil, especially when loose
earthworm: a long, thin worm that lives in the soil

The earthworm is a good friend. It eats leaves. It digs a tunnel in the dirt. An earthworm is little, but it can move dirt and it can move a big rock. It moves rocks and dirt to make tunnels. Rain and air go in the tunnels. Rain and air make plants grow.

We need the earthworm to help our food grow. Look where you walk after the rain. Do not walk on our good friend, the earthworm.

tunnel: an underground passage
rock: a large stone

Reading Comprehension

Answer the questions.

1. When and where should you look for earthworms?
2. What do earthworms do when it rains?
3. What does an earthworm look like?
4. Why do we need the earthworm?

Vocabulary

Collective nouns are words we use for groups of objects, animals or people. For example, a fleet of cars.

Match the collective noun to the group for which it is used.

a herd of	sheep
a flock of	bees
a swarm of	fish
a pride of	grapes
a platoon of	lions
a pack of	cows
a bunch of	cards
a school of	soldiers

Spelling

Read out the words and note how the **oo** words are pronounced.

oo has two sounds:

long o as in moon spoon too

short o sound as in wood book look

Circle the words that have a long o sound and underline the words that have the short o sound.

zoo	book	food	good	roof	cool	fool
hood	school	stool	tool	stood	broom	room
wood	loon	moon	noon	wool	cook	soon
foot	poor	goose	loose	boot	root	groove

Grammar

Classify the nouns in the table.

Praveena and Amit went to the market and got some flowers. They bought roses and lilies from the florist. Praveena arranged the flowers in a large clear glass vase. She put the vase on a table by the window. Anyone passing by the house could see the flowers in the window. The flowers were a cheerful and refreshing sight.

Name	Place	Thing

Punctuation

Correct the punctuation in the following sentences.

the boys in the neighbourhood had gathered outside for the usual cricket match in the evening one of the boys decided to show the others some fast bowling and the batsman decided to hit the ball hard the ball flew through the air right across the road it crashed into praveena and amit's window and smashed the vase the flowers were scattered all over the floor

Writing

Fill in the blanks with words from the text.

An earthworm does not have _______, legs or bones. It cannot make ___________. It does not have eyes, ________ or teeth. But it can ________through dirt and leaves and make __________. These tunnels let ______________ and water into the ground and help _______ grow. This is why the _____________ is considered our friend, because it helps us grow our _____________.

Listening

Follow the instructions you hear.

Speaking

Pretend you are an insect. Tell the class about your life.

Everyday English

Ordering food

Pretend you are ordering a Chinese meal from Hot Wok or an Indian meal from Maharaja's Durbar to be delivered to your house.

Take turns with your partner to be the restaurant person and the customer.

Activity

Make words by adding a letter or a group of letters to the word one. For example, someone (some + one)

Add the letters to the beginning, the end or both.

Use the picture clues given below.

________________ ________________ ________________

 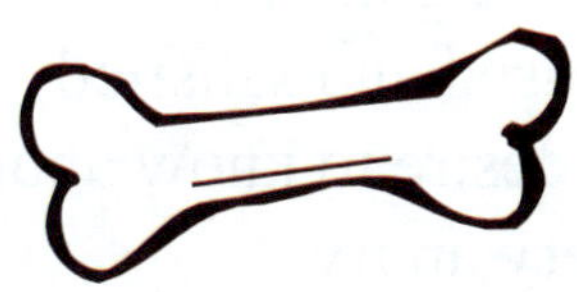

________________ ________________

4 Feelings

Risa Jordan

We each have feelings, me and you,
Sometimes we're happy and sometimes we're blue.

When something scares us, we feel afraid,
We all feel proud of something we've made.

When we want to know more, we feel curious.
When we slip on the floor, we feel furious.

We sometimes feel lonely when there's nothing to do.
We sometimes feel hungry when there's nothing to chew.

We all feel excited when we make a new friend,
I'm feeling sorry 'cause my poem must end.

---

blue: sad
afraid: fear of getting hurt
proud: pleased and satisfied
curious: a desire to know about something
furious: very angry
lonely: without friends
hungry: when you want to eat something
excited: happy
sorry: sad

RUMBLE

Reading Comprehension

Answer the questions.

1. Why do we feel afraid?
2. Of what are we proud?
3. When do we feel curious?
4. How do we feel when we slip on the floor?
5. Why do we feel lonely?
6. When do we feel hungry?
7. How do we feel when we make new friends?
8. Why does the poet feel sorry?

Vocabulary

We use special words to describe the manner in which animals move.

Unscramble the words below to describe animal movements.

1. snakes ielsrth ____________________
2. ducks aeddwl ____________________
3. horses oagllp ____________________

4. kangaroos ujpm __________

5. caterpillars awrlc __________

6. frogs oph __________

7. monkeys igwns __________

8. fish iwsm __________

Can you move like these animals?

Spelling

Use appropriate oo words to fill in the blanks.

root broom hood foot zoo moon room crook

1. She bought a new __________ from the market.
2. He hurt his __________ when he kicked the stone.
3. Look at the __________ in the sky.
4. Zahir saw many animals in the __________.
5. He ran outside the __________.
6. They cut and chopped the __________.

7. The raincoat came with a __________ to cover the head.

8. The thief was an old __________ who was known to the police.

Grammar

Some words, such as **is**, **am**, **are**, **does**, **do**, **has** and **have** are called **helping words** because they can be used with other verbs in a sentence. Helping verbs have no meaning on their own but help the main verb, which has the meaning.

Tick the correct option.

1. The boys (is/are) playing cricket in the playground.
2. She (has/was) wearing a new dress.
3. We (have/had) a party last week.
4. I (was/am) unwell yesterday.
5. He (had/is) the one with curly hair.
6. He (are/is) very busy.
7. She (is/am) reading a new book.
8. I (am/are) leaving now.
9. We (was/were) sad to see them leave.

Writing

Write a review of your favourite movie. You can use some of these words:

story actors funny happy sad scary long hero

What is the name of the movie? What language was it in? What is funny or interesting about it? What is the story all about? Which character did you like? Who are the actors that you liked?

Listening

Listen to the tongue twister. Repeat it slowly and then see how quickly you can say it.

Speaking

Describe your favourite movie to your partner and ask him/her about his/her favourite movie. Do you like the same kind of films?

Everyday English

Buying clothes

Take turns with your partner to be the shopkeeper and the customer as you shop for clothes.

Remember to ask about the size, the design, the colour and the price.

Activity

Back to front

Each of these words has its first part written last. Write each one correctly.

For example, gerfin is finger

daybirth	____________	eymon	____________
owyell	____________	eesech	____________
oonball	____________	terwin	____________

5 Rumours

One day, a hare was sleeping beneath a tree when a big ripe fruit fell down with a loud THUD! that shook the ground. The hare jumped up in surprise and started running. And as he ran, he shouted, "The earth is breaking apart! The earth is breaking apart!"

A deer saw the hare running. "What is the matter?" she

hare: a large rabbit that can run very fast

asked. "The earth is breaking apart!" said the terrified hare. And the deer too, began to run.

A rhinoceros saw the hare and deer running. "What is the matter?" he asked. "The earth is breaking apart!" they said. And the rhino, too, began to run.

A tiger saw the hare, the deer and the rhino running. "What is the matter?" she asked. "The earth is breaking apart!" they said. And the tiger, too, began to run.

A lion sleeping in a nearby cave heard the animals

---

rhinoceros: a large, heavy animal with very thick skin and one or two horns

thundering by. “What is the matter?” he asked. “The earth is breaking apart!” said the animals, panting for breath.

But the earth seemed quite solid beneath the lion’s feet. “Who started this rumour?” he asked the tiger. “It was the rhino,” said the tiger. “It was the deer,” said the rhino. “It was the hare,” said the deer. Then all the animals looked at the hare.

“It’s all true,” he said. “I heard the terrible noise with my own ears and felt the earth tremble.” Then he took them to the spot where he had heard the noise. Just as all animals reached the tree, another big ripe fruit fell to the earth with a loud THUD!

The lion laughed and said to the hare, “The earth isn’t breaking apart. You only heard this fruit hitting the ground.”

Then the lion said to all the animals: “This advice, I give to you. Don’t listen to rumours, they are often untrue.”

---

rumour: information that people talk about that may not be true

Reading Comprehension

Answer the questions.

1. What happened while the hare was sleeping beneath the tree?
2. What did the hare do?
3. Which animals saw the hare running?
4. What did the lion do to stop the animals from running?
5. What did the lion tell the other animals?

Vocabulary

Circle the odd word in each line. Say why this word is different from the others.

football	cricket	hockey	chess
potato	tomato	carrot	apple
rose	neem	tulsi	lily
whale	rabbit	hare	deer
tea	coffee	bread	milk

Spelling

Read out the words and note how ea is pronounced.

head sweat death deaf bread hear,
wheat meat bead weave leave

What is the difference in pronunciation when you use ea, ie and ee?

Choose the correct option to make the word.

1. p___ ___ ch (ae ea)

2. h __ __ d (ae ea)

3. b __ __ d (ei ea)

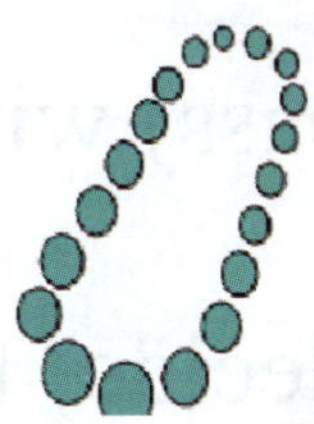

4. br __ __ d (ea ie)

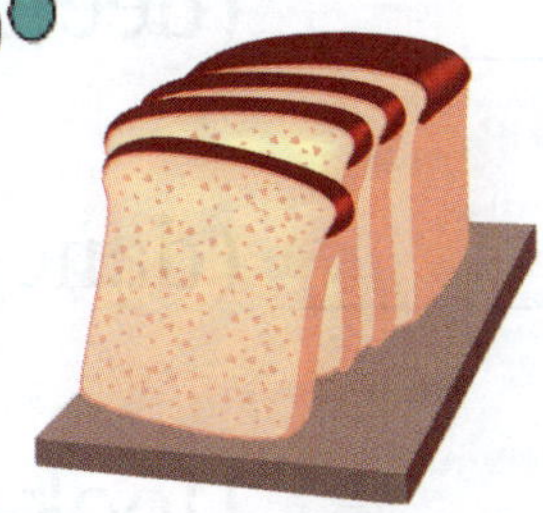

5. wh ___ ___ t (ae ea)

6. m__ __ t (ew ea)

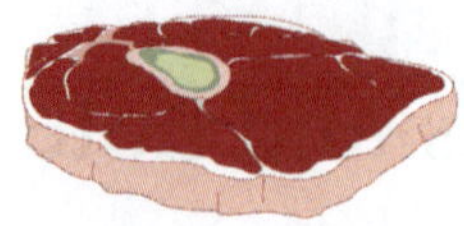

Grammar

We use the **past tense** to talk about something that took place some time ago. For example, we say "I watched a movie" when someone asks us what we did the day before.

Use -d or -ed to change the words in the bracket to the past tense.

1. Last summer I ____________(walk) for an hour every day.

2. He _____________(finish) his work before he left.

3. She ____________ (pass) with good marks.

4. We ____________ (decide) to go to the movies.

5. He _____________ (dance) very well at the show.

6. You _____________ (look) very nice at the party.

Find the past tense form of the words given in Box A. The past tense forms are given in Box B.

Box A		
buy	eat	bore
fall	lend	keep
say	ring	bind
come	do	sit

Box B		
kept	lent	sat
bored	bought	said
rang	ate	fell
bound	did	came

Punctuation

We use **exclamation marks** to indicate surprise, amazement or strong feelings.

Use capital letters and exclamation marks where required.

1. good morning india this is the daily news

____

2. wow we won the match against south africa

____

3. the dog ate the chicken that you wanted to cook

____

4. i don't like fruits or vegetables

____

5. go away stop trying to scare me

____

6. he didn't do his homework

____

Writing

Complete the letter in your own words.

Dear ____________________

Thank you so much for the ______________________________.

I have enjoyed it very much. ______________________________

____

Yours affectionately,

____

Listening

Try to guess the answers to the riddles you hear.

Speaking

If you know any jokes or riddles, recount them in class.

Everyday English

Making up a joke

What makes people laugh? Make up a joke and share it with your class.

Activity

Quick quiz

Read carefully and answer the questions.

Only Paula and Tina eat bananas.

Only Tina and Mira eat grapes.

Only Paula and Mira eat apples.

Who eats both apples and grapes? ________________

Who eats both bananas and grapes? ________________

What does Mira eat that Tina doesn't? ______________

What does Paula eat that Tina doesn't? ______________

6 The First Earnings

Vinita Krishna

On the southwestern coast of India is the little island town of Rameswaram. Many years ago, a little boy sat on the beach in the afternoons and dreamt of flying like the seagulls. This boy with wavy black hair and bright brown eyes grew up to be one of India's greatest scientists and the president of the country. This is an anecdote from the childhood of A.P.J. Abdul Kalam.

In April every year, during Ram Navmi, Rameswaram would be full of pilgrims from all across the country. For Abdul's family, this was a profitable time, for his father was a fisherman and a boat builder. His father would take pilgrims in his boat across to Dhanushkondi. On one such occasion, the shores of Rameswaram were struck by strong

pilgrims: people who travel to holy places for religious reasons
profitable: that which makes or is likely to make a lot of money
fisherman: a person who catches fish
boat builder: someone who builds boats
occasion: a particular time of an event

cyclonic winds. The family awoke to take stock of the wrath of nature. All their boats had been destroyed, which meant that there would be no income until they could build or buy new ones.

Abdul understood the need of the hour and decided to help earn money to support the family. He began to collect tamarind seeds after school for which he earned one anna (one sixteenth of a rupee). After seven days, Abdul took the week's earning and gave it to his father.

Abdul also helped his cousin, Samsuddin who had an agency for selling the newspaper *Dinman* in Rameswaram. Abdul would collect the newspapers from the railway platform, sort them and then hand them over to Samsuddin.

Abdul was happy that he had been able to contribute to the family income in its time of need.

---

cyclonic: when strong winds move in a circle; a violent tropical storm
wrath: extreme anger
nature: plants, animals and things that exist and are not made by humans
destroyed: damaged badly
income: money earned from work
tamarind: a very sour fruit
agency: a business organisation that provides a service to others
contribute: give money or goods or help

Reading Comprehension

Answer the questions.

1. At what time during the year do pilgrims visit Rameswaram?
2. What did Abdul's father do for a living?
3. Where did Abdul's father take the pilgrims in his boat?
4. What happened when strong cyclonic winds hit Rameswaram one year?
5. What did Abdul do after school to help his family?
6. What did Abdul do for his cousin, Samsuddin?

Vocabulary

Contractions are used to join two words, which sound shorter together. Common contractions include **I'm** (I am), **isn't** (is not) and **he's** (he is).

Write the shortened forms of the words below, putting the apostrophe in the correct place.

I have	______________	are not	______________
she is	______________	we are	______________
would not	_____________	was not	______________
does not	______________	will not	______________
cannot	______________	has not	______________
you are	______________	they are	______________

Spelling

According to the rules, we put **i** before **e** except after **c**. This means that when the letters **i** and **e** are included in a word, the **i** comes before the **e**, as in diet and alien. However, when the letter in question is **c**, **e** comes before **i** as in receive and deceive.

Read the words aloud and circle the misspelt words.

wield believe field ceiling conciet conceive teid receipt pie seive quiet peice

Find words that rhyme with the following words.

lapping flank lift kind note dumb tall stored

Grammar

The word **not** is used in a sentence to describe an action that is not taking place. For example, I am not eating.

Rewrite the sentences by adding the word not.

1. She was studying.

   ____

2. You have finished the jigsaw puzzle.

   ____

3. She is winning the race.

   ____

4. He has done his work.

   ____

5. They are playing together.

   ____

6. I have cleaned my room.

   ____

7. We are going to the market.

   ____

8. He is washing the car.

   ____

Punctuation

Correct the punctuation errors in the following paragraph.

when the cyclone struck rameswaram abdul's father's boats were destroyed this meant that the family would have no income until they were able to buy or build more boats abdul decided to contribute by collecting and selling tamarind seeds after school for which he earned one anna he also helped his cousin who had a newspaper agency by collecting the papers from the railway platform and sorting them out he was happy to help his father and family in the time of their need

Writing

Many children earn pocket money by working either before or after school. They look after children younger than themselves or deliver newspapers.

Describe ways in which children can help to add to the family income when times are difficult.

Listening

Listen to the conversation between a shopkeeper and a young girl. Then answer the questions.

1. What is the girl shopping for?
2. How much is the black wallet for?
3. Why doesn't the girl like the brown wallet?

Speaking

Share your favourite poem with your classmates.

Everyday English

Interacting with a visitor

How would you talk to someone visiting your home? Take turns with your partner to be the visitor and the host.

Activity

Why do the pilgrims visit Rameswaram on Ram Navmi? Find out more about it or about any other pilgrimage site.

7 Saving Grandma's Tree

Jey Manokaran

Chandri's Grandma was swept away in a flood of the Alaknanda River. Since then Chandri, who lives in a mountain village in the Garhwal Himalayas, spends many afternoons talking to the old ash tree and collecting firewood in the forests. Chandri and Grandma had often sat under the old ash tree on the mountainside.

One day as she sits on the tree and thinks of Grandma, Chandri hugs the tree and says, "You're my best friend."

---

flood: a large amount of water that covers an area
mountain: a very high hill
village: a very small town
firewood: wood cut into pieces that can be burned

Her thoughts are broken as the dusty trucks slow down to a stop.

Chandri runs back to the village and straight to her mother. She tells her mother that the men from the timber company have arrived with axes to cut down the trees.

Mother runs out to alert the neighbours. All the women of the village pick up their drums and like an army, march into the forest to save their trees.

"Chipko! Chipko! Chipko!" echoes through the woods. They explain that if the trees are cut the mountain, in the form of a landslide, will come down on the village. That is how the flood, which killed Grandma and two hundred others, happened. The landslide happened because so many trees were cut down.

---

thoughts: remembering something
timber: trees used to make things
alert: to warn somebody
Chipko: a movement where people hug trees to prevent them from being cut
landslide: mass of earth that falls down the slope of a mountain

"Hug the trees!" the women cry. Arms around the smooth bark, they clasp their hands together as they hold on to the trees. Chandri and the villagers cling to the trees, watching and waiting. The men look at each other and wonder what to do.

One man who had lost his mother in the flood throws his axe down.

One by one, the men troop into the truck and start the engines. The big boss reluctantly climbs in with them having lost a chance to get resin, timber and foreign exchange.

---

clasp: a firm grip, to hold tightly
reluctantly: with hesitation

Reading Comprehension

Answer the questions.

1. What happened to Chandri's Grandma?
2. Why does Chandri go to the forest?
3. What does she do when she sees the trucks coming to the forest?
4. What does Chandri's mother do?
5. What do the village women do to stop the men from cutting down their trees?

Vocabulary

Write the opposites of the words.

light	______________	night	______________
white	______________	fast	______________
soft	______________	hard	______________
ugly	______________	bitter	______________
cold	______________	down	______________

Spelling

Choose the correct word.

1. Do you (beleive/believe) what he told you?
2. The cows are grazing in the (field/feild).
3. The (ceiling/cieling) had cracks in it, through which the rainwater dripped onto the floor.
4. She was a rude and (conceited/concieted) girl.
5. Why did you (lei/lie) to me?
6. Do you have a (receipt/reciept) for the item you bought?
7. He ate a (piece/peace) of (pie/pei) after dinner.
8. The house was (quiet/queit) because the children had gone to school.

Grammar

Adjectives describe nouns and pronouns. They can tell what colour, size and shape something is. They can also tell how something sounds, feels or tastes.

Look at each underlined noun or pronoun. Circle the adjective or adjectives that describe it. Then write the adjectives on the lines provided.

1. My big brother likes to eat sweet, juicy fruits.

_________ _________ _________

2. He eats them on hot days. _________ _________

3. He cuts the red apple into four pieces. _________

____

4. Ripe bananas and juicy mangoes are his favourite.

_________ _________

5. Our loving Mom bought him a large, round watermelon.

_________ _________ _________

6. He made a colourful, delicious salad for all of us.

_________ _________

Punctuation

Rewrite these sentences using the correct punctuation.

dad and ravi have decided to make eggs for breakfast ravi is cutting up the onions and has tears running down his face dad is trying to beat the eggs he has spilled the eggs all over the kitchen and the tea has boiled over on the stove go away fluffy

i need a new dress but not in pink do you have this dress in another colour such as blue may i buy this black shirt also

Writing

Write questions for the answers given below.

1. Chandri's grandma used to go to the forest with her.
2. The timber merchants lost the chance to make money when the women did not let them cut down their trees.
3. The trees prevent soil from being washed away during the rain.
4. Trees also provide firewood for the village women.
5. Yes, that is why the women call the trees their friends.
6. No, the men do not stay behind in the village.

Listening

Listen carefully to the passage and draw the scene described.

Speaking

Talk to your partner using phrases, such as I could, I should and I would.

Everyday English

Saying goodbye

Talk to your partner using phrases that you use when saying goodbye.

Activity

Ask your parents and teachers about soil erosion and what can be done to prevent it. Write down three erosion facts.

8 The Swing

Robert Louis Stevenson

How do you like to go up in a swing,
Up in the air so blue?
Oh, I do think it the pleasantest thing,
Ever a child can do!

Up in the air, and over the wall,
Till I can see so wide,
Rivers and trees, and cattle and all
Over the countryside—

Till I look down on the garden green,
Down on the roof so brown—
Up in the air I go flying again,
Up in the air and down!

---

swing: a seat for swinging, hung from ropes or chains
pleasant: enjoyable
wide: measuring a lot from one side to the other
cattle: cows and bulls bred for their milk
countryside: land outside towns and cities
flying: going up

Reading Comprehension

Answer the questions.

1. What is the child doing?
2. As he swings himself high in the air, what does he see of the countryside?
3. What does he see of his own home as he swings back in?

Vocabulary

Read the words in this table. If you find that two words have the same meaning, you can colour both boxes the same colour. Use a different colour for each pair of words.

pull	sad	argue	unhappy
brave	smart	push	quarrel
follow	chase	tug	anger
shove	rage	courageous	clever

Spelling

Read these words aloud and note how u and ou are pronounced.

lung grunt stuck blush plump cousin slug tough fund young trunk rough

Grammar

> **Adjectives of degree** help us compare different objects, people or animals with each other. For example, He is taller than his brother, but you are the tallest.

Fill in the blanks using words from the brackets.

1. The cat is ____________ than the dog, but the mouse is the _____________. (small, smaller, smallest)
2. He is a _________ runner but she is the _____________ in class. (fast, faster, fastest)
3. Which is the ____________ mountain in the world? (high, higher, highest)
4. Grandma is _____________ but grandpa is _________________. (old, older, oldest)

5. She makes the ____________ food in the world. (tasty, tastier, tastiest)

6. Your feet are ___________ but hers are the ________________. (big, bigger, biggest)

Writing

Write an invitation to your birthday party. You need to include the date, the time and the address.

Dear ___________,

It's my birthday on ________________

I shall have a party that evening at __________ o'clock at ____.

Please do come. I look forward to seeing you!

Yours truly,

____

Listening

Listen to the groups of words. Identify the missing words.

Speaking

Do you have a pet? If not, have you seen any pets in your neighbourhood?

Talk about these pets to your classmates.

Everyday English

Describing a classmate

Describe one of your classmates to your partner, and have him/her guess who you are describing.

Activity

Name the things that you see when you go up in a swing in your playground.

______________________ ______________________

______________________ ______________________

______________________ ______________________

9 The Stick That Grew Shorter

Meera Uberoi

In a small valley surrounded by hills, there lived a zamindar in a big house.

One night, when all the villagers were asleep, someone crept into the zamindar's room. As the thief was leaving, the zamindar awoke and cried out, "What's that? Who's there?" But he only saw a flash of diamonds as the person ran out.

"Ramana! Raju! Help! Help!" The zamindar woke up the household and ordered the doors to be locked. The servants searched all over the house, but in vain. They informed the

---

valley: an area of low land between hills and mountains
zamindar: a landlord
thief: a person who steals from someone else
diamonds: clear precious stones
household: all the people living together in a house
servants: people who work in someone's house

zamindar that no one had left the house. The zamindar cried out in anger, “That means that the thief is one of you.” The following morning, the zamindar gathered all the

servants on the verandah. He gave one stick to each of them and warned the servants, "All these sticks are exactly the same length. Bring them back to me tomorrow morning. But the thief's stick would have grown by an inch."

That night Ramana could not sleep. He took a sharp knife and cut off an inch from his stick.

The next morning the servants returned the sticks to the zamindar. As soon as the zamindar saw Ramana's stick, he shouted, "Catch him! He's the thief!"

Ramana fell at the zamindar's feet. The zamindar told Ramana how foolish he'd been and that the trick to catch the guilty had worked. The zamindar said, "A stick doesn't grow unless it is on a living plant."

Ramana begged for forgiveness. He remained faithful to his master and never stole again.

---

verandah: an open, flat platform outside the house
foolish: unwise
trick: a clever act
guilty: the one at fault
faithful: supporting a particular person

Reading Comprehension

Answer the questions.

1. Where did the zamindar live?
2. When did the thief steal from the zamindar?
3. What did the zamindar see as the thief left his room?
4. Why did the zamindar order his servants to lock the doors?
5. What did the zamindar say when they were unable to catch the thief?
6. What did the zamindar do and say the next morning when he met both his servants on the verandah?
7. What did Ramana do at night?
8. What happened when the zamindar measured Raju's and Ramana's sticks?

Vocabulary

Homophones are words that sound the same but are spelt differently. For example, one and won.

Circle the correct word for each picture.

son sun 	for four 
see sea 	sale sail 
would wood 	
ear year 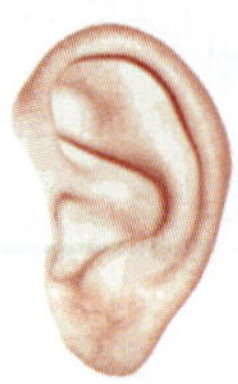	mail male

Spelling

Read the words aloud. Note the pronunciation of gh. Circle the words where gh is silent.

thought brought through fight eight bright right tough trough cough laugh draught

Grammar

> **Possessive nouns** are used to indicate that an object belongs to somebody. For example, instead of saying Fluffy is the dog that belongs to Meena, we say Fluffy is Meena's dog. An **'s** is used to indicate possession.

Rewrite the following using **'s**.

1. The necklace belonging to Tina

   ____

2. The mother of the boy

   ____

3. The house that Jack owns

4. The scarf that the girl wore

5. The stick that the man used

Punctuation

Rewrite these sentences using the correct punctuation.

1. ramana needed money to pay for his mothers illness
2. he was afraid to ask his master for money
3. he thought it would be easy to break into his masters room while he slept at night and steal the diamonds he kept in his cupboard
4. but when he did that his master woke up and ramana thought the master had seen him
5. ramana really got afraid when the master told raju and him that the thief had to be one of them

6. he gave them two sticks and told them that the thiefs stick would grow by an inch the next night
7. that night ramana cut his stick by one inch
8. and the very next day he was caught

Writing

Imagine you are the zamindar. Describe how someone stole from you and how you went about catching the thief.

Listening

Write down the sentences that are read out.

Speaking

Talk to your partner about your hobbies and ask him/her about his/her hobbies.

Everyday English

Asking for permission

Take turns with your partner to pretend to be the teacher and the student, and practice asking for permission.

Activity

Same letters

Two words in each line below have exactly the same letters in them. Circle these words.

ant	ate	sea	tea	flea
flow	hold	wall	wolf	ball
want	pant	wisp	wasp	paws
lame	lime	meal	make	sale
bake	tame	lake	meat	take

10 SOS! Let's Recycle!

Fay Robinson

Have you ever thought about how many things you throw out each day? At lunch, you may throw away your paper napkin, plastic or aluminium foil wrappers for sandwiches or paranthas, chips packets, juice cartons and fruit seeds and peels … the list goes on and on.

Imagine if every child from school throws away the same amount. That's a lot of trash!

Did you ever wonder where it all goes? First, trash from school gets loaded into large containers. Workers come by in

trash: things that you throw away because you no longer need them

garbage trucks to take the trash away. In many areas, they take it to a landfill—a large piece of land that has been set aside just for trash. A layer of dirt is spread over the garbage. This prevents the trash from blowing around and keeps animals away. Landfills hold a lot of trash. When landfills are full, they can be turned into parks.

Some areas have open dumps instead of landfills. Dumps are ugly and attract unwanted animals. Other areas burn their trash in huge furnaces called incinerators.

One of the best ways to reduce trash is to recycle. When you recycle something, all or part of it can be used again.

---

garbage: waste food, paper, plastic—all that is thrown away
dump: a place where large amount of waste is buried under the earth
incinerator: a closed container used to burn waste at high temperatures
recycle: to treat things that have been used so that they can be used again

Another way to help is to reuse things. Here are some ideas:

- Use both sides of the paper.
- Use cartons and empty boxes for art projects.
- Reuse plastic and paper bags.
- Don't buy things you really don't need.
- Use cloth napkins instead of paper ones.
- Always use your own shopping bag.
- Give away old toys and clothes instead of throwing them out.

Can you think of anything else you can do?

Reading Comprehension

Answer the questions.

1. What are the kinds of things that we throw away every day?
2. How is trash collected from your school or your home?
3. How is trash stored in a landfill?
4. How is trash stored in a dump?
5. What is recycling?
6. List the ways in which things can be reused.

Vocabulary

Some words, such as shoes and socks, go together.

Match the words given in Column A with the words given in Column B on page 83.

Column A	Column B
cup	cart
knife	key
horse	butter
bread	thread
lock	eye
brush	fork
hook	comb
needle	saucer

Spelling

Homophones are words that sound the same but are spelt differently. Note the differences in spelling.

rain/rein/reign	fair/fare
ore/oar	you/yew/ewe
rite/wright/right/write	bare/bear
pair/pear/pare	hare/hair
air/heir	

Tick the correct word.

1. Kavita and I went (two/to) the hotel last night.
2. I am going to (buy/by) a present for my mother.
3. I received a letter from my grandpa in the (male/mail).
4. The cat bit the dog on its (tail/tale).
5. Last (weak/week) we went to the beach.
6. Did you (here/hear) the roar of the jet?

Grammar

An **adverb** tells us more about a verb, an adjective or another adverb. There are adverbs of time, which tell us when something happens; adverbs of place, which tell us where something happens and adverbs of manner, which tell us how something happens.

Select adverbs from this list to fill in the blanks.

quickly quietly carefully softly swiftly
sweetly loudly proudly

1. She held the baby ____________.
2. The cheetah ran __________ after its prey.

3. We were late and we walked ____________.

4. She screamed _____________ when she saw the cockroach.

5. He walked __________ on to the stage to collect his prize.

6. We spoke ____________ in the library.

7. The children sang ___________.

8. He walked in ___________ because she was sleeping.

Punctuation

How would you write these sentences if you had to use these as slogans on posters? Rewrite these sentences putting in the correct punctuation.

1. use both sides of the paper

____

2. use cartons and empty boxes for art projects

____

3. reuse plastic and paper bags

____

4. dont buy things you really dont need

____

5. use cloth napkins instead of paper ones

____

6. always use your own shopping bag

____

7. give away old toys and clothes instead of throwing them out

____

Writing

Describe your best friend.

Listening

The sentences read out contain homophones. Write down the pairs of homophones. Take care to spell them correctly.

Speaking

Talk to your partner about what you did yesterday. Remember to use the past tense.

Everyday English

Clarifying information

Practice with your partner what you would say in situations when you have to ask someone to repeat something.

Activity

Make a poster about the 3 'R's—Reduce, Recycle and Reuse. Use catchy slogans such as 'Smash the Trash'.

11 Fishing

When I go fishing
I'm always wishing

Some fish will be my prize;
But while I'm fishing,
The fish are wishing
Otherwise.

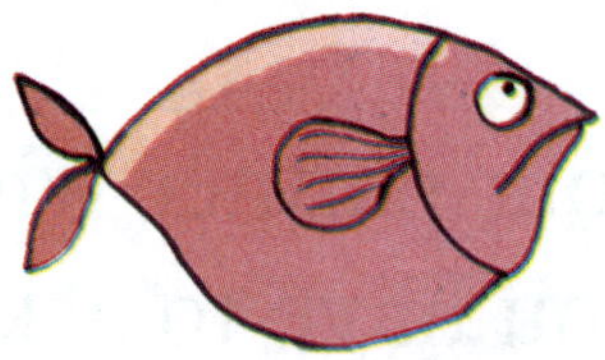

And all the wishes
Of all the fishes
Seem always to come true;
So all my wishes to catch some fishes
Never do.

wishing: to want something to happen or to be true
prize: award
otherwise: if something were not to happen

Reading Comprehension

Answer the questions.

1. What does the fisherman wish for when he goes fishing?
2. What do the fish wish for?
3. What happens every time he goes fishing?

Vocabulary

Unscramble the letters and label the pictures.

iauomtnn ________________

iadnls ________________

illh ________________

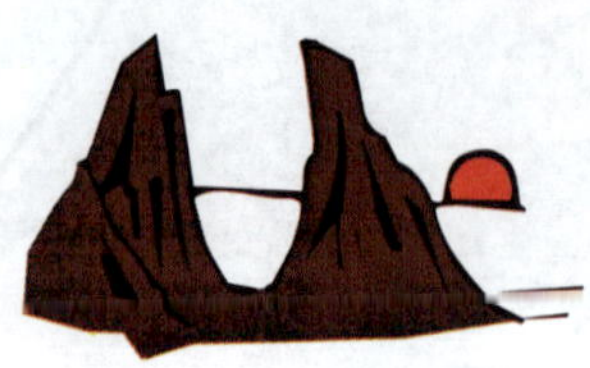

aellvy ________________

iffic ________________ ncaeo ________________

Spelling

Tick the correct homophone.

1. The (reign/rain) in Spain is mainly in the plains.
2. He found the (oar/ore) in the mine.
3. He wanted (too/to/two) go with the (too/to/two) of them for the movie.
4. I don't know how he can (bare/bear) to live in this (bare/bear) house.
5. She ate (pears/pairs) for breakfast.

Grammar

Adverbs tell us where an action takes place.

Use the words given below to fill in the blanks.

there everywhere outside inside away upstairs

1. They will play __________ the house.
2. I was ________ when it happened.
3. The bird flew ________ when the cage was opened.
4. Her bedroom is ___________.
5. You better come _________ before the rain starts.
6. She has a beautiful garden with flowers ____________.

Writing

Complete the letter to your grandparents.

Dear __________ and _____________,

How are __________? What is the __________ like? I have been ___________with school and my ___________. I have also been playing a lot of __________________. I have made many new __________________________________.

With love,

____

Listening

The sentences you hear contain words and their opposites. Write down the pairs of opposite words.

Speaking

Describe a place that you have visited. Where was it? What did you do there? When did you visit?

Everyday English

Taking a message

Pretend your parents are not at home and there is a phone call for one of them. You have to take a message. Take turns with your partner to be the caller and the child.

Activity

If you go fishing you may come across some of these sea creatures. Find the names of the following and colour them.

12 Moving Away!

Rohan and Rohit cannot believe that they have to move away from Bangalore. Bangalore is so fabulous! It's so wonderful. It's always been their home. They can play outside all day long—every day. It is almost always nice and sunny, and all of their friends live there. What will they do without Zahir, Raghav, Bunty and Vedant? They will never be able to make such great friends again.

However, Rohan and Rohit are very excited for their dad. He has a fantastic new job. The only problem is that the job is in a city way up in the mountains. In Shimla!

Shimla is the capital city of Himachal Pradesh. After learning that it is in Himachal Pradesh, near Chandigarh,

---

fabulous: extremely good
wonderful: pleasant, enjoyable
excited: happy and looking forward to
fantastic: excellent

both boys are excited about playing in the snow in winters. Rohit has always wanted to learn to ski, and Rohan thinks playing ice hockey will be great fun.

Rohan and Rohit also like the location of Shimla. Himachal Pradesh shares its borders with Punjab, Haryana

ski: to move on snow on long, narrow pieces of wood
location: place where a city exists

and Uttaranchal in the south and with Jammu and Kashmir in the north. The boys are keen to experience the ride on the toy train that passes through 102 tunnels. Neither of the boys has ever visited this part of the country, so they are looking forward to exploring the new place. If only their friends could come with them!

Their parents have promised that they can visit their old friends over the summer break and even invite them over to Shimla. The boys think moving to Shimla will not be so bad after all.

---

experience: observing, encountering or undergoing things
exploring: to travel and learn more
promised: to tell that something will definitely happen
invite: to ask someone to come over

Reading Comprehension

Answer the questions.

1. Where do Rohan and Rohit live?
2. How long have they lived there?
3. What is it that they like about Bangalore?
4. How is Shimla different from Bangalore?
5. What do the boys think they can do in Shimla?
6. What are they waiting to experience?
7. What have their parents promised them?

Vocabulary

Prefixes, such as **dis-**, **in-**, **im-**, **re-** and **ir-** are used to make new words. We use these to create the opposites of other words.

Circle the correct opposite of the first word in the list.

mature	inmature	dismature	immature
justice	rejustice	irjustice	injustice
comfort	imcomfort	discomfort	incomfort
responsible	irresponsible	disresponsible	imresponsible

possible	repossible	irpossible	impossible
ability	inability	reability	irability
regular	disregular	irregular	reregular
obedient	irrobedient	disobedient	imobedient
efficient	inefficient	disefficient	irefficient
mobile	dismobile	inmobile	immobile
sincere	insincere	dissincere	imsincere
action	inaction	disaction	reaction

Spelling

Read these words aloud. Note how o and au are pronounced.

plod drop cord short sport torn clock horde fort sauce haul pause fault haunt assault

Choose the correct letters to make a word.

f ___ ___ lt (au, ou)   r ___ w (u, o)

pl ___ d (u, o)   s ___ ___ ce (uo, au)

___ ___ to (uo, au)

Grammar

Pronouns take the place of a noun because we can use a pronoun, such as **his** or **her**, instead of a name.

Fill in the blanks with the correct words from the brackets.

1. This is _____ elder brother. (I/me/my)

2. This beautiful toy is _______ (you/your/yours).

3. ___________is wearing ___________new clothes. (Him/He, his/him)

4. Can ___________ borrow ____________ pen? (I/me, you/your)

5. ____________are going to ___________house. (We/She/Us, we/she/her)

6. _________will help __________with your work. (She/Your/Her, you/she/your)

7. This is ______house. (us/ours/our)

8. _______belongs to ________family. (It/Mine/I, my/I/mine)

Punctuation

Rewrite using correct punctuation.

1. moving house is not easy even if it is in the same city
2. it can be even more difficult when you move house between two cities
3. although bangalore is located far away from the sea it has a pleasant climate even in winter
4. in shimla it gets so cold in winter that it snows so you have to wear gloves and woollen caps sweaters as well as socks to keep yourself warm

Writing

Imagine you are Rohit or Rohan. Write a letter to your friends, telling them all about Shimla and how different it is from Bangalore. Write about the new school you have joined and your new home.

Listening

Listen carefully to the description of some things in the classroom. See if you can identify them.

Speaking

Talk to your partner about what rules you follow at home. What rules does your partner have to follow?

Everyday English

Disagreeing politely

Take turns with your partner to be the person who has made some rule and the person who disagrees with the rule. You must be polite and you must explain clearly why you think the rule is not right.

Activity

Rohan and Rohit have moved across the country. Make a list of the ways in which their lives will change. For instance, will they have to dress in warmer clothing during winter? Will they change schools? Will the games they play change? What are the other differences that you can think of between living in Shimla and Bangalore?

13 Outer Space

Carol Weston

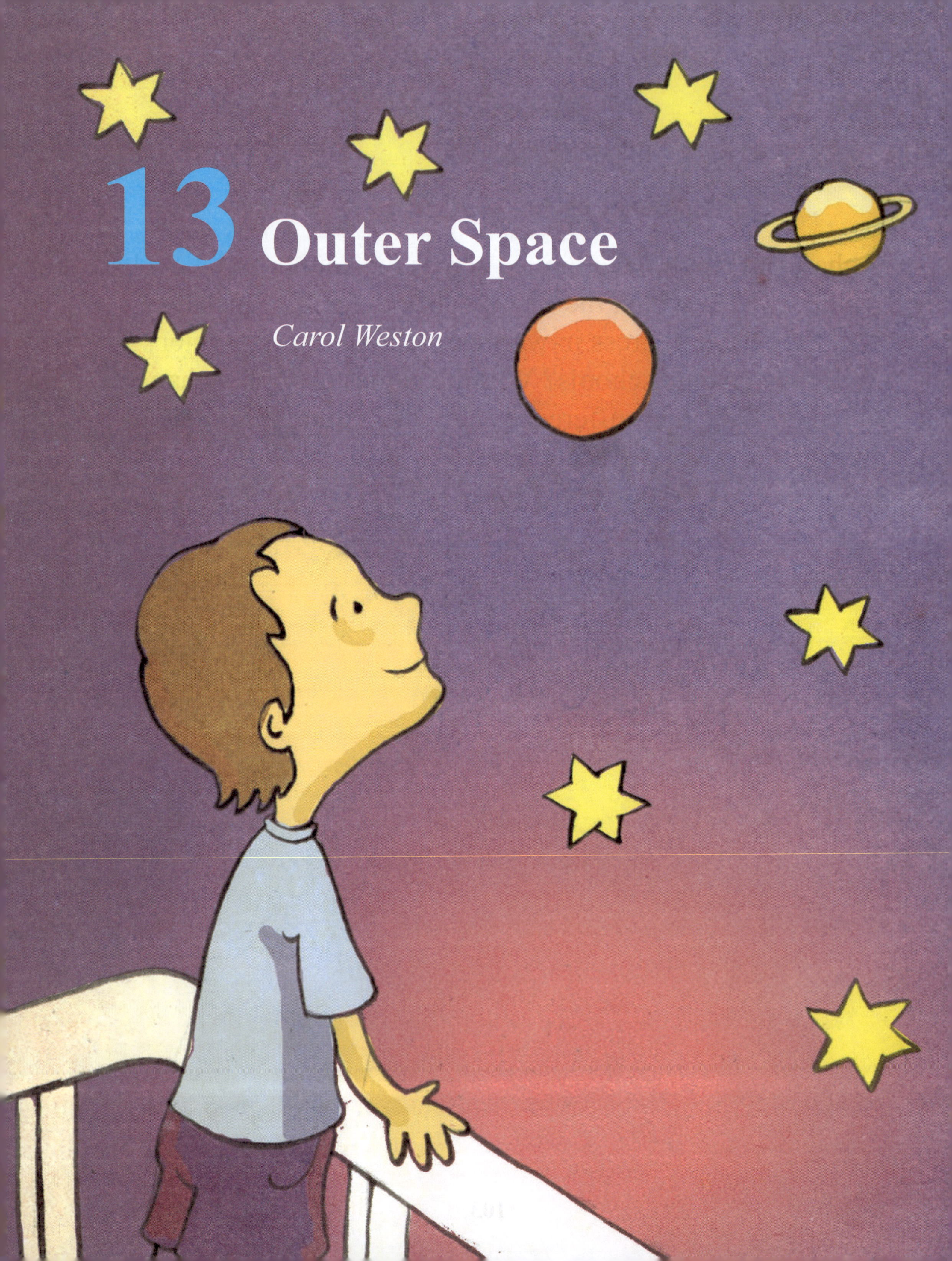

I look up from earth and try to see
The planets looking back at me.
I gaze at the bright and distant stars
And search for Mercury, Venus, Mars.
I squint at the Milky Way way up high
And look for Jupiter in the sky.
Where are Saturn, Uranus, Neptune?
They're far away, high like the moon.
A telescope would be the best
For spotting Pluto and the rest.
But even with my naked eye
I look for planets in the sky.

planets: a large, round object in space that moves around a star
distant: far away in space
squint: to look at something with your eyes partly shut to see better or keep light away
Milky Way: the galaxy or star system of which earth is a part
telescope: equipment used for looking at far away objects
naked eye: the normal power of your eye without the help of an instrument

Reading Comprehension

Answer the questions.

1. What is the poet doing by looking up from earth?
2. Where is the poet looking for Mercury, Venus and Mars?
3. Why is the poet squinting?
4. What instrument does the poet need to look at the planets?

Vocabulary

When we attach suffixes such as -**ful**, -**ness**, -**less**, -**ry**, -**ish** and -**ion**, the meaning of the word changes. For example, shy becomes shyness, bake becomes bakery and confuse becomes confusion.

What words can you create when you add the suffixes suggested?

1. boast + ful = ____________________
2. fool + ish = ____________________
3. attract + ion = ____________________
4. armour+ y = ____________________

5. rest + less = ____________________

6. beauty + ful = ____________________

7. fear + less = ____________________

8. soft + ness = ____________________

9. act + ion = ____________________

10. child + ish = ____________________

Spelling

Read the words aloud. These words have bt or pt in them.

doubt kept debt slept crept adapt adopt
septic leapt attempt swept wept rapt corrupt

Grammar

Prepositions show how a noun or a pronoun relates to the rest of the words in a sentence. For example, the box is on the table.

Use prepositions to fill in the blanks.

under over above below in out near beside

1. My diary is ________my pillow.

2. The newspaper is _______the car.

3. It is too hot to go _____________.

4. The stars are shining __________us.

5. Your room is _________mine.

6. I sit _________ her in class.

7. She held an umbrella ______his head.

8. The basement is _________us.

Writing

Imagine what it would be like to stand outside and look at the stars in the sky. Describe it in your own words. What can you see? How do you feel?

Listening

Identify the odd word from the list of words you hear.

Speaking

Talk about your favourite thing in nature.

Everyday English

Talking about your family

Talk to your partner about your family.

Activity

Find out why Pluto has recently been classified as a dwarf planet.

14 Time to Hibernate

Carol Pugliano-Martin

CHARACTERS:

Mr Mole

Squirrel

Squirrel: Hey Mr Mole! Where are you going?

Mr Mole: I'm going into my burrow. I'm going to hibernate.

Squirrel: Hibernate? What's that?

Mr Mole: I will sleep all winter. I will wake up in spring.

Squirrel: But you won't get to see the snow!

Mr Mole: You can tell me about it in the spring, Squirrel.

Squirrel: But you won't feel the cold air!

Mr Mole: You can tell me about it in spring, Squirrel.

---

mole: a small animal with dark grey fur that digs tunnels under the ground
burrow: a hole or tunnel in the ground
hibernate: to spend the winter in deep sleep
spring: the season between winter and summer

Squirrel: But you won't slide around on the ice!

Mr Mole: You can tell me about it in spring, Squirrel.

Squirrel: Mr Mole?

Mr Mole: Yes, Squirrel?

Squirrel: What is it like to hibernate?

Mr Mole: I'll tell you about it in spring, Squirrel!

---

slide: to move easily over a smooth or wet surface

Reading Comprehension

Answer the questions.

1. What does Mr Mole plan to do?
2. What will Mr Mole miss about winter?
3. When will Squirrel tell Mr Mole about sliding on the ice, or the snow and cold air?
4. When will Mr Mole tell Squirrel what it's like to hibernate?

Vocabulary

A **simile** describes something by comparing it to something else, using the words as or like. For example, as cold as ice.

Choose from the words given below to complete the similes.

thunder hawk feather fish pig ocean cucumber sky

1. as light as a ________________
2. as bluc as thc ________________

3. as loud as ________________

4. as cool as a ____________________

5. swims like a ___________________

6. eyes like a _______________

7. as deep as the ___________________

8. eats like a _______________

Spelling

Read aloud the adjectives and note the pronunciation.

delicious ambitious cautious superstitious infectious suspicious fictitious precious spacious nutritious gracious conscious

Note that the -tious and -ious words are pronounced in the same way.

Grammar

There are various kinds of sentences. An **imperative** sentence tells the listener to do something, a **statement** provides information and a **question** asks for information.

Circle the questions, put a cross (✗) against the statements and a tick mark (✓) against the imperatives.

1. What time is it?
2. It is four o'clock.
3. Close the window.
4. Please fetch me a glass of water.
5. Have you seen my diary?
6. Your diary is on the table.
7. Have fun at the picnic.
8. My brother lives in Delhi.
9. Finish your homework before you go to play.
10. Why hasn't Varun come to school today?

Writing

Which animals hibernate in winter? Find out about one of them and write a few sentences.

Listening

Identify the animals based on the descriptions you hear.

Speaking

Tell the class about your favourite season, and explain why it is your favourite.

Everyday English

Interviewing your partner

Your partner has just won a national competition. Interview him/her for the school newspaper.

Activity

Use the letters of the word HIBERNATE to make at least five small words.

How to Use a Dictionary

A dictionary is a book that lists the words of a language and gives their meanings.
People use a dictionary to find the meaning and the correct spelling of a word.
A dictionary also has some details about words such as their function or part of speech, their pronunciation, as well as origins or roots.
Other useful information, such as English to metric conversion tables, maps, explanations of common symbols, can be found in a dictionary.
There are separate dictionaries for languages, rhymes, slangs, idioms, geographical entries and medical terms.

*Let's start by locating the word **start**.*

Remember all words in a dictionary are listed in alphabetical order. This means that all the words beginning with the letter A are in the front and words beginning with the letter Z are in the back of the dictionary.

1. Open the dictionary so that it lies flat on the table before you.

2. Go to the pages that have words starting with the letter S. Scan through the words that are close to the first or first two letters of the word.

3. Notice the guide words at the top of each page. These words will guide you to the right page. The first guide word is the first word on a page, and the second guide word is the last word on the page. You can find your word between the two guide words.

4. You will now see all the words beginning with the letters st. Move to the third letter and keep moving down till you find the word start.

    Start (stärt) v. 1. to begin to do, be or happen. 2. begin to operate. 3. cause to happen or operate. n. 1. an act of beginning or the point at which something begins. 2. an advantage given at the beginning of a race. Phrases for a start in the first place. Start out (or up), begin a project or business. To start with as the first thing to be taken into account.

start¹ /stɑːt/ *n* **1(a)** [C] the beginning of a journey,
an activity, a plan, a race, etc; the process or an act
of starting: *make an early start (to one's journey)* ○
She behaved badly ***from start to finish.*** ○ *We won't*
finish the job today but we can make a start (on it). ○
I've written one page of my essay: it's not much but
it's a start. ○ *He knew* ***from the start*** *the idea was*
hopeless. **(b) the start** [sing] the place where a race
begins: *runners lined up at the start.* See also FALSE
START. **2** [C usu *sing*] an opportunity for or help in
starting: *give sb a fresh start* ○ *The money gave him*
just the start he needed. **3** [C usu *sing*] an advantage
gained or allowed in starting; the amount of this:
The smaller boys were given a start of 10 seconds in
the race. ○ *They didn't give me much of a start.* See
also HEAD START. **4** [C usu *sing*] a sudden quick
movement of surprise, fear, etc: *He sat up/woke up*
with a start. ○ *You gave me quite a start* (ie surprised
me). **IDM** **by/in fits and starts** ⇨ FIT⁴. **for a 'start**
(used in an argument) as a first point: *I'm not buy-*
ing it — I can't afford it for a start. **get off to / have**
a flying start ⇨ FLYING.
start² /stɑːt/ *v* ⇨ note at BEGIN. **1** ~ **(out)** to begin a
journey; to leave: [V, Vp] *We plan to start (out) at 6*
o'clock. [Vpr] *I started after her* (ie followed her) *to*
tell her the news. **2** to begin sth/to do sth; to begin to
happen: [Vn] *I start work at 9 am.* ○ *I had to start* (ie
begin using) *a new tin of paint.* ○ *He's just started a*
new job. [V.to inf] *It started to rain.* [V.ing] *He started*
laughing. [V] *I arrived after the play had started.* ○
I've had enough criticism for one day — don't 'you

If you can't seem to locate your word, make sure you are spelling the word right. You will not find the word honest under the o words.

Try using the word in a sentence. If it's difficult to spell, write it a few times to remember it.

Listening Texts

Lesson 1

Abby was sitting on a plump cushion in the drawing room. She was a big, grey cat with thick, soft fur and she loved to sit in this comfortable spot. No one else was allowed to sit on Abby's special cushion. Grandmother had told the children that they must not disturb Abby. So Abby was able to lead a happy and peaceful life, only leaving the cushion at mealtimes, when Grandmother would give her a delicious plate of food in the kitchen.

Lesson 2

1. This person serves food in a restaurant.
2. This person heals people who are ill.
3. This person grows food for us to eat.
4. This person flies planes.
5. This person writes books.

Lesson 3

1. Put your left hand on your right shoulder.
2. Stand up.
3. Turn to face the right.

4. Put both hands in the air.

5. Bend down and touch your toes.

Lesson 4

Sister Suzie's sewing socks for soldiers. Socks for soldiers sister Suzie sews. If sister Suzie's sewing socks for soldiers, where are the socks for soldiers sister Suzie sews?

Lesson 5

1. What comes thrice in December, once in February and never in March or April?
2. What comes up when the rain comes down?
3. What is the difference between here and there?
4. What breaks when you say its name?

Lesson 6

Shopkeeper : Hello! How may I help you?

Girl : Well, I'm looking for a gift for my father.

Shopkeeper : Okay. How about buying a new wallet for your father?

Girl : How much is that wallet?

Shopkeeper : Hmm … which one?

Girl : The black one.

Shopkeeper : Oh. It's for Rs 175.

Girl : That's too expensive for me. Do you have a cheaper one?

Shopkeeper : How about this brown leather one?

Girl : Umm … I don't think my father will like the design on the outside, and it doesn't have a place to put pictures. How much is it anyway?

Shopkeeper : It is for Rs 105 only.

Girl : Hmm. I don't have that much money.

Lesson 7

A small girl in a red dress is sitting on top of a big grey elephant. They are next to a blue lake with a purple boat in it. There are some green and brown trees. There are many yellow stars in the sky.

Lesson 8

1. Mercury, Venus, Earth, Jupiter, Saturn
2. ninety-four, ninety-five, ninety-six, ninety-eight, ninety-nine

3. April, May, July, August, September, December
4. spring, autumn, winter
5. Monday, Tuesday, Wednesday, Thursday, Saturday, Sunday

Lesson 9

1. Yesterday I shared an orange with my friend.
2. My sister is taller than my mother.
3. We dream when we are asleep.
4. My new bag is bright blue.
5. We have dinner at eight o'clock.

Lesson 10

1. Most people write with their right hand.
2. They had two clowns and an elephant too at the party.
3. Have you seen the lamb that belongs to that ewe?
4. We paid the entry fare and went on all the rides at the fair.
5. In my bag, there is a pair of gloves, an apple and a pear.

Lesson 11

1. She was happy to go to Spain but sad to leave her friends behind.
2. He had a bath with hot water because it was a cold day.
3. Turn on the light—it is too dark to read.
4. These shoes are tight but the others are loose.
5. I will climb up and throw the ball down.

Lesson 12

1. It is made of paper and has lines inside for us to write on.
2. It is made of wood, has four legs and we sit on it.
3. It is made of wood, has four legs and we put our books on it.
4. It is black and we use chalk to write on it.

Lesson 13

1. belly, tummy, stomach, arm
2. run, sprint, walk, dash
3. mud, soil, grass, earth
4. sad, glad, happy, joyful

5. write, read, jot, note

Lesson 14

1. It is big, covered with fur, with orange and black stripes.
2. It is very big and grey with a long trunk and tusks.
3. It lives in China, is black and white and eats bamboo shoots.
4. It is small, lives in houses, has long whiskers and a tail and is afraid of cats.
5. It lives in the desert, has a hump on its back and can go without water for many days.

Acknowledgements

The publishers would like to thank the following for permission to use copyrighted material:

Baaraan Ijlaal for the illustrations for 'Time to Hibernate'; Jey Manokaran for 'Saving Grandma's Tree' from *Saving Grandma's Tree* (Scholastic India: 2006); Meera Uberoi for 'The Stick That Grew Shorter' from *Why the Wagtail Is So Tiny and Other Folktales* (Scholastic India: 2006); Partha Sengupta for the illustrations for 'Saving Grandma's Tree'; Priya Kuriyan for the illustrations for 'We are One World', 'Rumours', 'The Swing', 'Outer Space', 'Fishing' and 'Feelings'; Priyankar Gupta for the illustrations for 'Moving Away'; Scholastic Children's Books UK for 'Best Friends' from *Charlie and the Rocket Boy* by Hilary McKay (Scholastic UK: 2008) and the accompanying illustrations by Sam Hearne; Scholastic Inc for 'We are One World' by Meish Goldish, 'Fishing', 'Feelings' by Risa Jordon, 'Outer Space' by Carol Weston from *A Poem a Day* (Scholastic Inc: 1997); 'After the Rain' from *Scholastic Success with Reading Comprehension and Fluency Grade I* (Scholastic Inc: 2004) by Mary Rose; 'Rumours' from *Round-the-World Folktale Mini Books* (Scholastic Inc: 1995) by Maria Fleming; 'SOS! Let's Recycle' from *Rookie Read-About Science: Too Much Trash* by Fay Robinson (Scholastic Inc: 1995); and 'Time to Hibernate' from *25 Emergent Reader Plays Around the Year* by Carol Pugliano-Martin (Scholastic Inc: 1999); Shweta Mohapatra for the illustrations for 'After the Rain'; Uma Krishnaswamy for the illustrations for 'The Stick That Grew Shorter'; Vinita Krishna for 'The First Earnings' from *A Boy and His Dream* (Scholastic India: 2006); and Zainab Tambawalla for the illustrations for 'The First Earnings'.

While every attempt has been made to trace copyright holders for the text, illustrations and photographs, this has not been possible in all cases. Any omissions brought to our attention will be rectified in future editions.

